Katherine E. (Katherine Eleanor) Conway

On the sunrise slope

Katherine E. (Katherine Eleanor) Conway

On the sunrise slope

ISBN/EAN: 9783741161278

Manufactured in Europe, USA, Canada, Australia, Japa

Cover: Foto ©Andreas Hilbeck / pixelio.de

Manufactured and distributed by brebook publishing software (www.brebook.com)

Katherine E. (Katherine Eleanor) Conway

On the sunrise slope

ON THE SUNRISE SLOPE.

BY

KATHERINE E. CONWAY.

WITH INTRODUCTION

BY THE

REV. PATRICK CRONIN.

NEW YORK:
THE CATHOLIC PUBLICATION SOCIETY CO.
1881.

Copyright, 1881, by
KATHERINE E. CONWAY.

TO MY

FATHER AND MOTHER,

THIS BOOK IS DEDICATED,

BY THEIR LOVING CHILD

THE AUTHOR.

CONTENTS.

INTRODUCTION
LOTUS AND LILY
BEFORE THE CROWNING
THE FIRST RED LEAF
IN THE DESERT
THE SONG OF THE EVERGREEN TREE
STORM-STRICKEN
TWO VINES
MARY LEE
GOING TO BETHLEHEM
ANOTHER JUNE
THE HEAVIEST CROSS OF ALL
ESTRANGED
DISENCHANTED
GOOD-BYE
A STORY'S ENDING
FOREBODINGS
IN MEMORY OF LENA

CONTENTS.

	PAGE.
FERNS FROM WATKINS GLEN	70
NEPENTHE	72
NEW YEAR, 1879	73
IN EXTREMIS	76
TO MY FRIEND	79
A NEW OLD SONG	80
MAGDALENE	82
TO MY DEAR FRIEND, ANNA FRANKLIN O'RIELLY, FOR HER MARRIAGE-DAY	85
CROWN AND PALM-BRANCH	87
REMEMBERED	89
A SONG IN MAY-TIME	91
BLOOMING OUT OF TIME	94
MY BROTHER'S BIRTHDAY	95
A BIRTHDAY GREETING	99
TRUCE	101
A PRAYER OF SHADOWED HEARTS	102
A LIFE'S REGRET	103
RENDING THE VEIL	104
VANQUISHED	105
THE WOODLAND FLOWER	109
WEEP NOT	112
THE GOLDEN BIRD	113

CONTENTS.

	PAGE.
THE ROSEBUSH AND THE ROSE	114
GOOD-NIGHT	115
AT OUR MOTHER'S SHRINE	119
CHOSEN	122
CHRIST IN THE WILDERNESS	124
"STAR OF MY DYING-TIME"	126
OUT OF SWEET MEMORIES	128
ELECTA	130
MY FATHER'S HOUSE	132
A SPIRIT'S MESSAGE	134
A CHILD OF MARY'S PRAYER	135
SUMMER LILIES	137
"BEHOLD, THY KING COMETH"	140
FORGIVEN	143
IN THANKSGIVING	145
SISTER MARY BERNARDINE	147
AN ALTAR-LAMP	149
AD MAJOREM DEI GLORIAM	151
IN SIGHT OF HOME	157

INTRODUCTION.

YIELDING, at last, to the importunities of friends, Miss Conway has consented to publish this little volume of selections from her poems which have already won public favor in several of our Catholic periodicals. Not more than half of her verse productions are gathered here; for, on entering into the critical world of authorship, she has exercised too severe a censorship, and excluded from this literary casket, many a gem of rare worth, which, in the opinion of the present writer, would give additional charm to this collection. But these we hope to have at no distant day; for, doubtless, with the courage and confidence born of success, Miss Conway's mystic muse will soar on bolder wing, and add many a poetic sister to this eldest born, that now so bashfully makes her *début* on the literary stage.

Stranger readers will, no doubt, regret that there is not prefixed to these pages some portrait of the author, so that admiring her song they could sometimes turn in sympathy to gaze on the face of the singer. The writer shares this regret ; and were Miss Conway, instead of being connected with this UNION office—in which her labors are of a most unpoetic nature—either afar with one sister under alien skies, or peacefully sleeping with another—of whom she so sadly sings— under these April violets, he would venture to supply the omission, albeit with rude pen picture. But she is here—here daily, over dreary, weary work ;— and her singularly retiring spirit and maidenly modesty restrain his pen.

Under these circumstances, all he would say is that Katherine E. Conway is second daughter of James Conway, a once wealthy citizen of Rochester, now a resident of this city. Casually, and in a literary way, the present writer first met Miss Conway, she having kindly contributed to the UNION some of the poems that now appear in this volume. She was then—as she is now—shy and sensitive in the extreme, and deeply pained at the slightest word of praise. Gifted with rare facility of composition, both in prose and verse, the varied products of her accomplished pen are scattered like the Sybils' leaves ; and not until the sea gives up its dead shall the world know all she has anonymously written in the cause of Religion, Charity and Truth. And when we, the while, recall the fact of her almost continued wretched health ; the many strains inseparable from a highly nervous organization ; the self-imposed task of wrestling with literary labor far into the night, for several periodicals ; the delicate conscience that in all things so rigidly rules her life ; and the sublime spirit of self-sacrifice that so heroically shines forth in her every act ; some idea may be formed, by readers of these poems, of the mental and spiritual complexion of their author.

The writer will not stop to express any critical judgment, or to point out what he regards as singular beauties in these specimens of Miss Conway's verse. Anything he could say on this head, would scarce influence the taste of the reader. Besides, such analysis would lead him far beyond the bounds prescribed to this introduction. He would merely say, in brief, that, in his opinion, the chief charm of these poems lies in their exuberant spontaneity. They bubble up fresh and clear as a sparkling spring; and, like the stream that flows therefrom, murmur their way, full sweet and low, through green fields and fragrant foliage resonant with the untaught melody of the wild bird's song.

As with most persons into whose souls the divine *afflatus* has been breathed, there is a tinge of melancholy in Miss Conway's verse—not indeed a dark wail of despair; but a tender sadness, not seldom the twin sister of religious genius, which fancy loves to picture on the pale nun's face, who sighs to go hence beyond the stars.

Alas! too often poetic genius proves a fatal gift to its possessor; and the inspiration of the Muse seldom brings contentment to the heart or blessings to the life. Unfortunately, the heritage of many of those thus endowed is little else than a continued rosary of sad sighings; a ceaseless looking backward to days that are no more; quivering lips, and a stretching out of pale hands to clasp the poor ghosts of unrealized dreams. But when Religion attunes the lyre, and keeps the breathings of passion subject to its purifying influences, then indeed the poetic faculty is a celestial boon; it hath a noble mission to spiritualize and elevate; and whilst its exercise serves to soothe the longing soul of the singer, the numbers of his inspired song inflame the heart of the hearer with the fadeless charms of imperishable Truth, Beauty and Goodness. So long as these three sisters of the skies shall visit earth, so long shall poets be born to chant their loveliness; and the sordid money-seeker, who, in his unglutted greed, would wholly materialize the world, had as well try to hush the blackbird's song on the fragrant hawthorn, as hope to silence the poet's hymn of praise over the glorious works of God.

Buffalo, April 23, 1881.   PATRICK CRONIN.

LOTUS AND LILY.

ON THE SUNRISE SLOPE.

LOTUS AND LILY.

SOMETIMES a dark hour cometh for us who are bound to bear
The burden of lowly labor, the fetters of lowly care.

An hour when the heart grows sick of the workday's weary round,
Loathing each oft-seen sight, loathing each oft-heard sound!

Loathing our very life, with its pitiful daily need;
Learning in pain and weakness that labor is doom indeed.

And this the meed of the struggle:—tent, and raiment and bread?

O for the "Requiescant," and the sleep of the
    pardoned dead!

O the visions that torture and tempt us (how shall
    the heart withstand!)
The fountains, the groves, the grottoes, of the
    Godless Lotus-land!

O the soft, entreating voices, making the tired
    heart leap,
"Come over to us, ye toilers, and we will sing ye
    to sleep."

A fatal sleep, we trow! but we are sad unto
    death,
And the Lotus-flower unmans us with its sweet
    and baneful breath.

We look to our fellow-toilers—what help, what
    comfort there?
They're bowed 'neath the self-same burden, be-
    set by the self-same snare.

Falleth the ashen twilight—meet close for the
    dreary day;
Hark to the chimes from the church-tower! —
    but we are too tired to pray.

Ah, God, who lovest Thy creatures, sinful, and
    poor and weak,
Hear'st prayer in the tired heart's throbbing,
    though the lips are too tired to speak?

Is this Thy answer? Is this the herald of Thy
    peace?
For the Lotus withers before him, the songs of
    the Syrens cease.

And the palm trees and the grottoes, fountains
    and streamlets bright,
Waver and change as he cometh, then fade from
    our weary sight.

He is worn with care and labor; he is garbed in
    lowliest guise,

But we know the firm, sweet mouth, and the
    brave, brave, patient eyes;
And we know the shining lilies—no blooms of
    mortal birth—
And we know *thee*, blessed Joseph, in the guise
    that was thine on earth.

Thy hands are hardened with toil, but they have
    toiled for him
Upon whose bidding waited legions of Seraphim.

Thy hands have trained to labor the hands of
    Him who made thee,
Whose strength upbore thy weakness when thy
    awful trust dismayed thee.

O lift thy hands in appealing for us who, un-
    willing, bear
The burden of God's beloved, lowly labor and
    care.
O pity our fruitless tears, to-night, and our hearts
    too tired for prayer!

BEFORE THE CROWNING.

BEFORE THE CROWNING.

LO, it draweth near the midnight! shine the stars or lower the skies
Where the lordly domes and turrets of my father's dwelling rise?

Doth he pace the lofty terrace, gazing on the gloomful water?
Doth he yield one thought of pity to his doomed and prisoned daughter?

O my father! O my kindred! pity in your hearts hath perished;
Ye have spurned me, ye have scorned me —me whom late ye proudly cherished.

Even as of old the scoffers spurned and scorned in wanton pride

Him for whose dear sake I suffer, my Beloved,
   the Crucified.

Hearts of flesh are turned to iron, by mine own
   flesh am I hated,
In my maiden blood to-morrow shall the tiger's
   thirst be sated.

For, say ye, I've shamed my lineage, wrought
   for ye undying sorrow—
O my dear ones, all *my* grief dies with my dying
   on the morrow!

Even now within the arena stand I bound, my
   dread doom biding,
Myriad bright eyes, keen and cruel, gaze on me,
   my woe deriding.

Ah, but fiercer eyes transfix me, round and red,
   with fury glaring!
Hark, a roar! Ah, God, the tiger! hot breath
   burning, sharp fangs tearing!

* * * * * *

O Beloved, save me, spare me, Thou who art
    divine and human!
Thou who knowest mortal weakness, spare me —
    I am but a woman!

Not like glorious Cecelia, not like brave Perpetua
    dowered!
Nor the blessed child, sweet Agnes, strong where
    manhood might have cowered.

Yet, like them, I too would love Thee; for Thy
    sake the worst would bear;
But to-night my shuddering heart can only
    moan—In pity, spare!

I have braved my father's anger, scorned for
    Thee fond Nature's urging,
Given my body to the rack —yea, even to the
    shame of scourging.

Now I'm faint with deadly faintness, blood from
    all my wounds is streaming,

But the pain outlasts the languor —would 'twere death, and not death's seeming!

Ah, Thou knowest I would be true to Thee —Beloved, hear my cry,
Here, amid the dark and silence, I implore Thee, let me die!

Lest, perchance, when sorely tempted on the morrow I should falter,
Let this prison-floor to-night be for Thy victim as an altar.

Send Thine angel Azrael to comfort me with balm of death—
Prone in fear and pain behold me, bid me yield this struggling breath.

* * * * * *

In the moonlit olive-garden, prostrate in His agony,

Prayeth Jesus: "O my Father, let this chalice
    pass from me!

Hear my prayer, my God, my Father, hear the
    voice of Thine own Son:
Yet, my God, if I *must* drink it, not my will, but
    Thine, be done."

Thus with burning lips He prayeth from His
    crushed and bleeding Heart,
While the sweat of hot red blood-drops forth
    from every pore doth start.

From the moonlit olive-garden floateth out His
    voice to me:
"O my dear one, my predestined, I would share
    my cup with thee!

'Tis a bitter draught, my dear one, unto lips and
    heart a-thirst,
And I pity all thy shrinking —ere I gave thee, I
    drank first.

But the hour is nigh when thou mayst look on my
unveiled face.
Lo, mine angels compass thee, and thou art
clothed with my grace!

Wilt refuse the cup? wilt leave me, thou, mine
own, my promised bride;
Thou whose lips but yesterday my name 'mid
tortures testified!"

* * * * * *

Lo, 'tis past! again the silence and the pain and
prison-gloom;
But no more the wild, wild terror:—welcome,
welcome, blessed doom!

In God's strength I will be strong, the wrath of
men and devils braving;
In His love I will be meek —but ah, to know my
blood they're craving!

Hush, proud heart! O Mother Mary, plead, lest it
    from Heaven delay me?—
O forgive me, Lord, forgive me, and—forgive
    their sin that slay me!

BUDS AND BRIERS.

THE FIRST RED LEAF.

IT gleams amid the foliage green,
While earth is fair and skies serene:—
A little, fluttering, scarlet leaf,
The herald of a coming grief.

It saith to summer—Even so.
Thy fading-time is near, I trow;
And I am come to whisper thee
Of gloomy days that yet must be.

A little longer wear thy crown,
Nor lay thy blooming sceptre down
And in the sun's benignant smile
Forget thy fears a little while.

I shall not see thee pass away—
Swift is my coming, brief my stay.

Scarce doth the blessed daylight shine
On beauty shorter-lived than mine.

But know that thou art past thy prime:
It draweth near thy fading-time —
I am the herald of thy grief,
The first red leaf, the first red leaf.

IN THE DESERT.

THE sand is hot beneath my tired feet,
    No shade of spreading tree nor vine is near,
Nor sound of smallest brooklet rippling sweet
    Breaketh the awful silence reigning here;—
And the stern sun from his meridian throne
Glareth upon the desert vast and lone.

Ah, once through forest and through field I strayed,
    And friends were with me—we sang out in glee,
Until the birds with answering voices made
    The bright day ring with blithest melody!
I was so happy —and no shadow chill
Fell o'er my path to bode of coming ill.

Could it have been a dream as brief as fair,
    The vanished glory of those early years?—

And have I wakened unto truth and care,
    To sorrow and to suffering and to tears?
Memory or dream—which?—oft I scarce can
    tell—
O fare thee well, forever, fare thee well!

Ah, me! how long the days are and how dreary
    The while I'm wandering in this unblest
    land,
And all in vain, till I am faint and weary,
    Seeking for foot-prints in the trackless sand!
And O to think the cool, green paths I trod
But led me here at last, my God, my God!

THE SONG OF THE EVERGREEN TREE.

I FEAR not the keen and searching breath
    Of the merciless winter wind,
As the pitiful wrecks it scattereth
    That autumn hath left behind.

And the storm may beat with relentless stroke,
    But my green, green robe I'll wear,
While birch and maple and elm and oak
    Are shuddering, brown and bare.

O desolate winter, hail to thee!
    Hail to thy frost and snow!
Dearer, far dearer, they are to me
    Than the summer's bloom and glow.

O weave me a robe of feathery white
    Over my robe of green!

And make it bright by day and by night
    With the frost-gems' pearly sheen.

A wild, wild gladness awakes and lives,
    Thrilling and trembling in me,
And a voice to the song of my heart it gives—
    Winter, I welcome thee!

STORM-STRICKEN.

To M. E. C.

THY sister trees are crowned
　With wealth of leafage, green, and fresh,
　　　and sweet,
　　Casting unto the ground
Their cool, broad shadow in the summer heat.

　　And many a little nest
Beneath their boughs is built with tender care,
　　Where downy birdlings rest,
And with impatient twittering fill the air.

　　But now no more to thee
Will the birds come and in thy branches sing —
　　Nor ever wilt thou be
Laden again with snowy blossoming.

It is not ruthless time ·
Whose sure, unsparing hand hath left thee so,
    For thou wert in thy prime
Of strength and beauty, one brief moon ago.

    But swift and sudden came
A blight on thee in wind and storm and gloom—
    Blasting with lightning-flame,
The promise of thy white and fragrant bloom.

    And now, thou art alone
Lifting thy bare dead branches to the sky,
    And making desolate moan
Unto the heedless winds that wander by!

June, 1871.

TWO VINES.

BY the garden-gate sprang a flowering vine,
    And it sprouted and strengthened in shower
        and shine.

It reached out tendrils on every side —
There was none to prune, there was none to guide.

So it wavered and fell from its tender trust
And trailed its bright blossoms down in the dust.

Within the garden its sister-vine
O'er many a friendly branch did twine.

Both were fed with the same sweet dew,
Both in the same kind sunlight grew.

But one was tended with fondest care,
And its blooming gladdened the garden fair:

While the other as fragrant and pure and sweet
Was trodden under by passing feet.

Days go by till the summer is fled,
The year is waning, and both are dead.

MARY LEE.

SHE was but a little child,
  Pure and innocent and mild,
Love's lone blossom in the wild.

O my little Mary Lee,
Thou wert God's good gift to me,
God knows how I cherished thee!

O how long is life's delay!
O the long years passed away,
Since my darling's dying-day!

Soon, full soon, the story's told:
I again my love behold,
Heart-throbs hushed, all marble-cold.

Leaving love's bright page unread,
Tears love bringeth all unshed,
Words of love unthought, unsaid.

O my little Mary Lee,
Thou on earth couldst never be
What thou art in Heaven to me!

And my love for thee was pure,
Else it could not so endure,
Cradled in my heart secure.

Chaste and tranquil and serene,
Upward-tending, passion-clean,—
So we love God's saints I ween.

I had wandered far away,
Into darkness out of day,
Lured by phantom-lights astray.

Little good was left in me,
Save thy holy memory,

My undying love for thee.

But within me woke a yearning,
Tearful, tender, softly burning,
For the dear days unreturning.

And my heart went seeking thee,
Through the realms of mystery,
My lost darling, Mary Lee.

Soon the clouds began to break;—
Did the dear Lord pity take
On my soul for thy sweet sake?

Even so it might have been;
Veils thyself and me between,
Many mysteries surely screen.

Ah, no matter what betide,
Now I care for naught beside
So my Lord be glorified.

When the light of morn is clearest,
And the thought of Heaven is nearest,
Then my lost one seemeth dearest.

O my little Mary Lee,
Thou on earth couldst never be
What thou art in Heaven to me!

GOING TO BETHLEHEM.

SHINE out, sweet Star, in the heavens afar, as
    once in the past you shone!
For I'm out in the night—the cold, dark night—
    on a journey long and lone;
And lost, as the distance groweth, like the thought
    of an old-time dream,
The lights of the home that once was mine, no
    more on my pathway gleam.

On, through the grand old city—my unseen guide
    and I—
And the doors of happy homes swing wide, the
    while we hasten by;
And the glimmer and glow they woo me to rest
    beside the way,
And sweet, sweet voices sue me—but I dare not
    pause nor stay.

On—on! will the rest come never! the city is far behind—
Brighter the light of my Star above, keener the winter wind.
O I am chilled and wayworn, and I fain would lay me low.
And slumber soft in that fleecy drift of the white and stainless snow!

Fewer and wider severed the wayside hamlets rise,
Now—naught but the snow-clad untracked waste, meeteth my longing eyes.
Courage, faint heart! remember, like the chosen of old thou seekest
The dwelling-place of the Promised One and His Maiden-Mother meekest.

Shine out, fair Star, shed thy beams afar, o'er my pathway wild and lone—
For quenched to-night is all earthly light that erst to cheer me shone!

Nerveless and weak are my fettered hands that
    once were firm and strong—
How long ere my faltering feet may rest? sweet
    Spirit, say, how long?

*   *   *   *   *   *

Hark! on the midnight breaking, to the chime
    of viewless bells,
To the far-off song-burst waking, that louder and
    sweeter swells!
While high in the bluest heaven burneth my
    blessed Star,
That hath drawn me away with its pure, soft ray,
    from earth's wavering lights afar.

What though I'm weary, breathless—my journey's
    end is nigh,
And the childish plaint of my spirit faint into
    stilly peace doth die;
For here is the Shrine and Shelter—a lowly rock-
    hewn cave—

Of the King who is sure to pity; ready and strong
    to save!

I praise Thee, Lord, for Thy radiant Star—Thy
    gift of measureless worth—
It hath led me out of my foolish dream of the
    bitter-sweets of earth,
To the resting-place of the King of Grace—my
    Saviour and Thy Son—
Now, one step more through the opening door,
    and I know my Heaven begun!

ANOTHER JUNE.

To M. A., Convent Sacred Heart, Rochester.

LAST June, in my lone garden, a lovely rose tree grew,
Rich in God's gracious giving of sunshine and of dew;
Rich with a wealth of roses, fragrant and glowing red.
"I ween there are none fairer in all the world," I said.

E'en as I spake a spirit came to my humble door,
I trembled gazing on him—oft had he come before.
"Give me the roses, maiden;" his voice was calm and sweet—

"Give me these cherished blossoms ere cometh
    noontide heat."

"Nay; wouldst thou claim the roses? I've given
    all the rest;
Whate'er thou wouldst I gave thee, the rarest and
    the best.
Leave me these last sweet blossoms, my lonely
    life to cheer—
Leave them, I pray thee, leave them; to me
    they've grown so dear."

Murmured the spirit sadly, "O maiden, need I
    tell
Who bids me claim the roses—thou knowest all
    too well;
Yet keep the flowers thou lovest, that I in vain
    implore."
Then the sweet spirit vanished, and came to me
    no more.

ANOTHER JUNE.

Ah, me! my red, red roses: they bloomed for many a day;
At last the summer waned and died, and then they passed away;
Yet my heart sang within me, "Grieve not, for thou wilt soon
See thy red roses budding when comes another June."

Another June! alas! alas! behold, sweet June is here!
But June hath brought no roses my lonely life to cheer;
Never a bud nor leaflet to glad mine eyes again—
My rose tree fair is withered—only the thorns remain.

1874.

THE HEAVIEST CROSS OF ALL.

I'VE borne full many a sorrow, I've suffered many a loss —
But now, with a strange, new anguish, I carry this last dread cross;
For of this be sure, my dearest, whatever thy life befall,
The cross that our own hands fashion is the heaviest cross of all.

Heavy and hard I made it in the days of my fair strong youth,
Veiling mine eyes from the blessed light, and closing my heart to truth.
Pity me, Lord, whose mercy passeth my wildest thought,

For I never dreamed of the bitter end of the
    work my hands had wrought!

In the sweet morn's flush and fragrance I wan-
    dered o'er dewy meadows,
And I hid from the fervid noontide glow in the
    cool, green, woodland shadows;
And I never recked as I sang aloud in my weird
    and wilful glee,
Of the mighty woe that was drawing near to
    darken the world for me.

But it came at last, my dearest,—what need to
    tell thee how?
Mayst never know of the wild, wild woe that my
    heart is bearing now!
Over my summer's glory crept a damp and chill-
    ing shade,
And I staggered under the heavy cross that my
    sinful hands had made.

I go where the shadows deepen, and the end
    seems far off yet—
God keep thee safe from the sharing of this wo-
    ful late regret!
For of this be sure, my dearest, whatever thy life
    befall,
The crosses we make for ourselves, alas! are the
    heaviest ones of all!

ESTRANGED.

A BARRIER hath risen between
   Thy heart and mine, O friend, I ween—
Cruel and strong, though all unseen!

We made that barrier, thou and I,
And strengthened it as days went by;
Ah, me! I scarce know how or why!

Mayhap, some promise given and broken,
Some word unkind, though lightly spoken;
Then, hearts that grieved but gave no token.

Farewell! O loyal heart and true,
How wouldst thou pity if thou knew
The mazes that I wander through,

As wider, wider, every day
Our paths diverge!—O friend, I pray
That thine may be the sunnier way!

I, in my lone lot, scarce could pine,
While *thou* wert quaffing life's red wine,
E'en though its bitterest cup were mine!

DISENCHANTED.

THY sad tears unchecked streaming,
    Sick of thy selfish dreaming,
Thou turn'st from old enchantments wearily,
    O child, hath aught but losing
    Come of thine idle musing?
Hath it wrought anything but pain for thee?

    Ah, how could thy desire
    Rise holier and higher
Seeking its treasure and its rest above;
    While tranced with soft regretting
    Strong purposes forgetting,
It languished o'er wild dreams of earthly love!

    What dark place have they brightened,
    What heart sore-laden lightened,

These floating fancies of thy restless brain?
    What spirit hath grown stronger
    To trust and suffer longer,
Thou, waking thoughts of Heaven to soothe its pain?

    O blessings scorned and wasted!
    O cup of peace untasted!
O gracious guerdon thou hast left unwon!
    Still grieving thine own losses,
    Counting thy little crosses,
And singing thine own woes from sun to sun!

    No longer dream-enchanted,
    No longer shadow-haunted,
O child, have done with words and wishes vain!
    For oh, hath aught but losing,
    Come of thine idle musing?
Hath it e'er wrought thee anything but pain?

GOOD-BY.

MY little darling! for a short, sad space
   I fold thee in a clinging, close embrace,
     And read the limpid depths of thy dark eyes;
Knowing full well that never, never more
Wilt thou be to me what thou wert before,
     For, with this dying day, our old life dies.

Think not my love for thee is less, sweet child,—
Else would it follow thee with yearning wild?
     And losing thee, would life have deeper gloom?
Or would unshed tears burn, because I know
That I must let my budding lily go
     That other hands may tend it till it bloom?

What though we part with lingering, fond regret,
Thou, in thy fair new life, mayst soon forget

  Her whom to-night thou callest loved and
    dear;
For others in soft tones will breathe thy name,
And hold thy young heart's love with surer claim,
  And wiser counsel give, and holier cheer.

Yet some day, when this heart, so frail and lone
Hath, with the long years' struggles, stronger
    grown,
  Perchance we'll meet in trust serene and
    high;
And find it ours, that joy so blest and strange—
Of love too pure to suffer any change—
  May God so will it, darling!—now good-by!

A STORY'S ENDING.

MY pleasant, perilous straying all is done—
O Father, save Thy wilful, wayward one!
Erewhile, alas! I fled from Thine embraces,
And now, I'm lost in lone and thorny places!

I slighted Thy dear love unchanging, tender,
For an ambitious dream's inconstant splendor;
Nor heeded gathering briers—fading day—
As if a dream could light my life for aye!

Out of my need, I pray,—who erst prayed never—
Cast not Thy faithless one away forever;—
Pity my disappointment and my pain,
And my poor, empty life, so vain, so vain!

The strong, sharp thorns on every side close round
    me —

Thy justice, too long scorned, hath surely found
    me!
The storm-wind shrieketh—whither can I flee?
O come, all pardoning Love, and rescue me!

FOREBODINGS.

SNOW through the valley drifteth drearily,
    And snow enshroudeth all the hills to-night;
O'er wastes of snow winds wander wearily,
    And snow-clouds threatening shut the stars
        from sight.

There broodeth o'er my heart a heavy dread,
    Colder and drearer than the sullen snow;
And darker than the dun clouds overhead,
    As the night deepeneth, my forebodings
        grow.

If I could only tell my fears in words,
    Or to my dear ones picture them to-night,
They would fly from my heart as dismal birds
    Fly from the coming of the holy light.

But who hath lived and loved, and never known
    Some fears so much his own that none could
        share them,
Some griefs that must be hidden—borne alone—
    All earthly aid too weak to help him bear
        them?

So, veiled, my pitying God, from all save thee,
    I guard my sad forebodings—friends would
        chide them—
But Thou rememberest Thy Gethsemane,
    And in Thy loving Heart Thou bid'st me hide
        them!

IN MEMORY OF LENA.

Died June 8, 1875.

O YE virginal white rose buds, all dewy, sweet
    and tender,
Swaying on your frail, frail stems, though ne'er a
    breeze doth blow;
I love ye for that fairer bud that perished 'mid the
    splendor
Of the song and sun and fragrance two summer-
    tides ago!

I called her oft our rose bud—no flow'ret's name
    seemed meeter,
For the pure and joyful promise of her lovely,
    girlish grace;

But past my art to picture—than all my dreaming sweeter,
The glorious, wondrous spirit-light upon her fair young face.

O the baleful fever-breath our fragile blossom blighting!
O the bitter chalice to our darling's young lips pressed!
O the fitful gleams of false, false hope awhile our darkness lighting!
O the days and nights of agony and woful, wild unrest!

But the Lord Himself was with her to pity her and love her;
Earthly lover shared not her maiden heart with Him,
And the gentle Virgin Mother and the Angels bent above her,

And their glory round her brightened as the lights
of time grew dim.

My friend, my chosen sister—child and woman
strangely blended—
Did thy spirit go out gladly, leaving blessing as it
fled?
For all its living loveliness thy face in death transcended,
Purer than the snowy blossoms o'er thy virgin-
vesture spread.

O heart that loved me loyally, that prized my
poor endeavor,
If I loved thee purely, truly, I would be glad for
thee!
But O my life without thee! Lord of the bright
forever,
Forgive my plaint who knowest what my darling
was to me!
  1877.

FERNS FROM WATKINS GLEN.

EMERALD-TINTED, purely glowing,
In the cool depths of the dim glen growing;
Hid from the beam that scathes and burns,
Slender, trembling, delicate ferns,
How ye glad with your timid graces
Lonesome clefts in the rough rock-places!

Shrink ye warily, bending lightly,
As the chill spray-shower gems ye brightly.
Do the gay butterflies bring ye stories
Of the far hill-tops' sunny glories?
Or greetings blithesome and full of love
From sister-ferns in the woods above?

* * * * * * *

Over the rocks the wild brooks leap,

Brave vines cling to their foothold steep,
Bracing breath from the pine-trees thrills us,
Weird and wondering gladness fills us,
While we gather ye, ferns so purely glowing,
In the cool depths of the dim glen growing.

NEPENTHE.

THY sweetest memories perish,
    Thy bitterest remain;
How long, how long wilt cherish
    Dark dreams of bygone pain?

O the wisdom of forgetting
    Which the burdened heart should crave!
O the folly of regretting
    What regret no more can save

Look to the coming splendor,
    Thou on the sunrise slope,
Nor thus to Memory render
    The tribute claimed by Hope.

NEW YEAR. 1879.

I PRAYED last night, full oft and passionately,
  The while the sad Old Year drew near its death,
"Lord, let the sorrow that o'ershadoweth
This life of mine now drift away from me.
O let it pass, Lord, with the passing year,
And let the morrow dawn in peace and cheer!"

A few there are who love on nights like this,
In dream or speech to live dead years again,
Because no shadow of reproachful pain
Vexeth their memories of by-gone bliss.
But, O my darling, I am not of these,
Nor dared I yield the night to memories!

O I have had my joys;—the ecstasy
Of youth and blameless loves —but how be glad,

E'en though my past hath not been wholly sad,
Knowing what lies between its joys and me?
Yes; through a mist of hot, remorseful tears,
I must look back upon my happy years.

Dost know, dear child,—(but wherefore shouldst
    thou know?)
That oft what we call blessing is our bane,
And sweetest pleasures yield the sharpest pain?—
Live, little one;—thou, too, mayst prove it so.
And yet, I would not weep to suffer more,
Couldst thou go safe where I've been wounded
    sore.

O the sad night, by dread forebodings haunted!
The while I wept and craved the long desired;
But at the last, I slept—I was so tired—
Before the requiem that the church bells chanted,
When the Old Year gave up his last faint breath,
And his weak hands grew chill and white in
    death.

NEW YEAR, 1879.

O sweet to sleep, forgetting!—Gray and cold
The wintry dawn in through my window gazed,
And sudden I awoke, with dreaming dazed ;—
Ah me! ah me! in vain the requiem tolled!
For there, between the morning light and me,
Stood my old sorrow, smiling pitilessly.

What use to moan or fret?—Too late, alas!
O poison-fruit, from idly scattered seed!
O bitter sequence of a careless deed!
The year hath passed —but wilt thou ever pass?
Or wilt thou grow of all my years a part,
And hourly with thy strong hands wring my
    heart?

Have mercy! I have sinned, O blessed Lord,
And even so must suffer; let it be!
But O forget my long disloyalty,
And peace, the peace of Heaven, at last accord.
And teach my heart to love this darksome guest
Who bideth with me at Thine own behest.

IN EXTREMIS.

Dying! who says I am dying?—Come here, come close to the bed,
Look at me—don't speak in whispers;—there's worse than death to dread.
I'm weak, but that is the pain; and O this fluttering breath!
But 'twas often the same before;—it surely is not death.

Raise the curtain a little; it can't be dusk, I know,
For I heard the bells ring noontime scarcely an hour ago.
Why are you here alone?—'Tis passing strange indeed,
If there's none but you to tend me in my saddest, sorest need.

Only a year since I came here, a proud and happy bride,
Scorning for you all else on earth —yea, and in Heaven, beside;
False to the Faith of my fathers, my childhood's blessed Faith,
And all for the short-lived love of a man—and now the end is death.

Is this fast-ripened harvest too bitter for your reaping,
That you stand like a very woman, wringing your hands and weeping?
You love me?—Would I had never listened to lover's vow!
What is your love to me if it cannot help me now?

Pray?—Do *you* bid me pray?—A seemly counsel, ay,
Sweet prayer! ah, not for me!—Do you know what it is to die?

Do you know my rending pain!—this chill fast-
 gathering gloom?
Or my helpless, desperate fear of the Judgment
 and the Doom?

Mock me not with your tears! O leave me—
 don't you see
How I yearn for the light, and all the while you
 are keeping the light from me!
The love that we called undying in this awful
 shadow dies:
O lost, lost years when I craved no light but the
 baneful light of your eyes!

Hark to the rushing of wings!—O shapes of
 horror and dread,
What would ye have of me that ye crowd around
 my bed?
Closer, closer!—Ah, God,—but in vain I cry to
 Thee,
Even as I forsook Thee hast Thou forsaken me!

TO MY FRIEND

O WILL that gift men call success,
    Bring the same joy to me?
    No, no; this failure's memory
Will e'er make after-triumphs less.

The loss is mine, the pain is mine,
    And mine to mourn a failing power,
    And know it failed me in the hour
It might have eased a care of thine.

A NEW OLD SONG.

I PRAY as men have prayed since earth was young,
 In varied voice or speech—a prayer of pain;
I sing—ah me, the song is ever sung!
 And ever more, as now, in vain, in vain.
'Tis O to be a little child once more,
 A little, lowly child, dear God, I pray!
I would give all my life has yet in store,
 Could I retrace my childhood's rosy way.

O cruel, questioning eyes, so keen and bright!
 O cruel, all-revealing noonday sun!
How can I choose but shudder at the light,
 When I have only wrecks to gaze upon!
O for the long, long shadows of the morn!
 (The sun shone only on high places then,)

To veil me or from pity or from scorn!
    Would God I were a sinless child again!

How can I choose but mourn my lost estate
    Of brave emprise and white, untroubled trust,
The palace of my dreams made desolate,
    My king uncrowned, my treasures turned to
        dust!
O tell me not that life has much in store!
    Can it give back what once I cast away!
But O to be a little child once more—
    A little, lowly child, dear God, I pray!

MAGDALENE

I HAD no share in the Christmas cheer,
   Nobody wished me a happy New Year.

Vain the wishing—how could there be
A happy New Year on earth for me?

O dear Child Jesus, I pray Thee take
Pity on me for Thy Mother's sake.

She 'mong women most high, most blest,
And I the lonest and lowliest.

She all sinless and pure—but I—
Ah, would I could shrink out of sight and die!

For mine own vileness affrighteth me!
And my prayer is the moan of my misery.

O dear Child Jesus, *Thou* hast forgiven,
But the world sees not with the eyes of Heaven.

On me it layeth the weight of blame,
Mine is the exile and pain and shame.

But Thou hast mercy for me, and care—
I know it, I trust it, else my despair

Would rise in its strength and burst for me
The awful gates of Eternity.

Would that the shame were mine alone!
Would the sorrow were *all* mine own!

But alas for the home whence joy hath fled!
Where they who love me have wished me dead.

The poor old mother who pines heart-broken,
The sisters who blush if my name be spoken!

Comfort them, Lord, for their fond hopes crost,
Comfort them for their dear one lost!

Faded and thin is my golden hair,
Wan the face that was erst called fair

Dimmed with weeping the eyes once bright—
O short-lived summer of sin's delight!

All my glory hath fallen from me
As the leaves in June from a blighted tree.

Who but God could pity or bless
A wreck thus left to its wretchedness!

TO MY DEAR FRIEND ANNA FRANKLIN O'RIELLY.

For Her Marriage-Day.

SOFTLY and tenderly,
   More fond than gay,
Wakes my heart's wish for thee,
   Sweet friend, to-day.

Through pleasant, peaceful ways,
   We walked together,
In childhood's merry days
   Of April weather.

Our friendship never knew
   Chill doubts nor tears;
But firmer, fonder, grew
   With flying years.

And dearest, this bright morn,
    My friend, art thou,
While bridal-blooms adorn
    Thy gentle brow.

Heart-prayers hath Heaven heard
    For thee, sweet friend;—
May light, fore'er unblurred,
    Thy steps attend.

And all good gifts be thine:—
    In vain, I seek
In these poor words of mine
    My wish to speak!

CROWN AND PALM-BRANCH.

In Memory of Frances Mary McManus.

FOLDED in raiment fair and white,
  Blossoms about her, dewy and bright,
Palm-branch laid on her peaceful breast—
Sweet, O sweet, is the maiden's rest;
But the loving watchers mourn and weep;
For this is *death*, though it seemeth *sleep*.

She hath done with earth-life—the strange, sad story—
She hath seen the face of the King in His glory,
She hath drunk of the river whose wave is balm,
And the virgin's crown and the victor's palm
Are hers forever:—no fear, no pain—
  O who would call her to earth again?

And thus we muse of the captive freed,
And thus would comfort the hearts that bleed—
The hearts sore-wounded and nigh to break—
While they look on that sleep so fair to see,
And moan—" Ah, yes; it is well with thee;
But O Beloved, if thou couldst wake!"

Buffalo, Palm Sunday, 1880.

REMEMBERED.

REMEMBERED thus, my dearest! remembered! can it be
That, after all my waywardness, I'm still so dear to thee?
Though changed thy outward seeming, that thy heart no change hath known,
And the love I thought had left me is still my own—my own?

O *I* remembered! but I said, "I, too, can be unheeding."
With smiling eyes and aching heart I stilled sweet memory's pleading—
Or dreamed I stilled it—murmuring, "Soon shall my strength atone

For the cares and joys he shares not, and the
    triumphs won alone."

One word from thee, beloved, and the pent-up
    fount's unsealed,
And all my self-deceiving to sense and soul revealed,
And all that lonesome, toilsome past clear-pictured unto me,—
O it never had a day, dear, unlit by prayer for
    thee!

Fore'er divided?—yea, for earth; but our lives
    have wider scope,
And the bonds between us strengthen with our
    strong supernal hope.
For oh, my friend, my dearest, how God's love
    halloweth
This love that, unaffrighted, looks in the face of
    Death!

A SONG IN MAY-TIME.

A SONG for the joyful May-time,
    A song like the song of a bird,
A song of the heart in its play-time,
    With never a sorrowful word!

A song—but whence shall I win it?—
    Winged like the butterflies,
With the fresh-leaved woods' breath in it,
    And the glow of the glad sunrise!

This is the song you ask, dear,—
    Would I could do your will!
But, set we a song as a task, dear,—
    A test of the singer's skill?

A dweller in cities ever,
    A toiler within the walls —

A SONG IN MAY-TIME.

'Mid the tumult of man's endeavor,
    Where the unseen fetter galls;—

Little I know of the tender,
    Blithe songs that the free birds sing,
Little I know of the splendor
    Of the wild wood's blossoming;

And less of the heart's sweet play-time—
    So brief was mine, you know;—
And the flowers of my beautiful May-time
    Died under a strange; late snow.

Out of my life the cheery,
    Sweet spirit of youth is fled;
My songs are the sighs of the weary,
    Or plaints for my dear ones dead.

Yet, you've loved this sad song-voice, dear,
    You would give it a nobler range,
And because of your honor and choice, dear,

'Twere fain to ring out and rejoice, dear,
    With the mirth of the May-time change.

O joy to be your joy-bringer—
    When 'tis joy, dear, even to pray
That a fairer and gladder singer
    Will sing your song of the May!

BLOOMING OUT OF TIME.

POOR flow'rets of the springtime that bloomed
  not in your season,
 Unseemly your unfolding 'mid the summer's
  royal cheer!
The sweet, red roses question—and, I ween, with
  amplest reason—
 "O me! our frail, pale sisters—but wherefore are ye here?"

Hide your wan, wan faces, the radiant roses
  shame ye!
 Blush for your belatement as mortals blush
  for crime!—
But O my shy, sad flow'rets! can I have heart
  to blame ye?
 Must I crush your tender lives out for blooming out of time?

MY BROTHER'S BIRTHDAY.

O IF I had a royal gift
   To lay in thy dear hands to-day!
And O if I had power to lift
   Whate'er of thorns may strew thy way;
And from thy life's fair heaven bid drift
   Even the tiniest cloudlet gray!

But, granted. When the end drew nigh,
   Wouldst love me for my foolish prayer?
Wouldst look to thine untroubled sky,
   And read thy future's glory there?
Or shrink, and murmur drearily,
   "She's lost me life's divinest share?"

Ah, well! no royal gift is mine,
   Nor power to win thee what I would:

I can but seek the Altar-shrine
    (My clamor of desire subdued)-
Wherein abideth the Divine,
    Changing life's gloomful chance to good.

Not gold, I pray. The hour-glass runs,
    And youth is fled, and gold is dross.
Nor love, that 'neath these alien suns
    So blooms, that oft our love is loss.
Hush, pleader!—with His dearest ones
    Christ shares His Chalice and His Cross.

So, may God's will be done in thee,
    His angels have thee in their care,
His power between thy foes and thee,
    His blessing with thee everywhere;
Hark! holier lips implore for thee,
    But never breathe a different prayer!

August 29, 1880.

SONNETS.

A BIRTHDAY GREETING.

To * *

MY friend, dear friend, I hail the morning's beam,
    Full fain to send thee greeting, fain to pray
    For brightest blessings on thine own bright day—
For joy that is—not joy that doth but seem.
What shall I pray? What I, short-sighted, deem
    The best and sweetest, might be seed of pain.
    What shall I pray? Ah, well I know 'twere vain
To give a voice to my desire or dream;
For Eyes Divine look down and read it right.
    Sometimes we live to weep a granted prayer;

So I would have God choose my prayer for thee,
    for thee,
That it may find sure favor in His sight
    And win for thee some gift surpassing fair
    And fadeless—even in Eternity.
1879.

TRUCE.

STAY, thou art tired; thy Father bids thee rest.
    Tarry awhile beneath the palm-trees' shade,
    Eat of the fruits around thee, unafraid,
Drink of the limpid stream His hand hath blest,
After the sore, sharp struggle comes a guest,
    Sweet Peace, with respite even as thou hast
        prayed.
    Rest, till refreshed and with new strength
        arrayed—
To face the old-time perils. Short at best,
This welcome truce. Yet linger not, but swift
    Go forth when thou art summoned, else I fear
        Thy joy will turn to grief; the hot, red
        sand
Over the delicate flowers will drift and drift
    And choke the stream, now purling crystal
        clear,
    And change the garden to a desert land.

A PRAYER OF SHADOWED HEARTS.

THE grief, long dreaded, nears us. Mother, see!
   How the weird shadows hide the sun's warm
      glow!
   Ah, by thine own unutterable woe,
When the sharp sword of Simeon's prophecy
Rended the veil 'twixt Calvary and thee,
   And then transpierced thy soul;—(for, even so
     Our shrinking and our shuddering dost thou
      know!)
Comfort us with thy pity motherly,
And make us wise in time. Too oft, alas!
   The mercy of God's sword we would not see,
     Nor His supreme love-token in the Cross,
We blindly let the hours of sorrow pass
   Void of fruition for eternity,—
     The while the wondering angels wept our
      loss!

Feast of the Purification, 1880.

A LIFE'S REGRET.

O LONG-LOST friend, what have I harvested
   Of thy youth's bloom and mine, with its delight
   Of love and laughter and fore-runnings bright?
Not peace, not hope, but life-long pain instead.
Sometimes this sleepeth, till I dream it dead—
   When lo! a word, a look, a soft drawn breath,
   And into fullest life it wakeneth,
Ah, me! unrested and uncomforted
For all its sleep. How could I let thee stray
   Into the vale of death, thy torch unlit,
   And mine ablaze that might have kindled it?
O wnat befell thee on that fearsome way?
   And O what greeting would be thine to me
   Could thy voice reach me from eternity?

RENDING THE VEIL.

I THOUGHT that white veil hid a sacred shrine;
    That the clear flame thus glimmering through could rise
    Only from fire of purest sacrifice
Lit from the Lord's own Altar. It was mine
To dream fair tracery of sheaf and vine
    Upon that baffling veil which jealously
    Shrouded what I was yearning for. Ah, me!
How many a blessed day did rise and shine
On my vain dreaming.—Well, I dream no more
    Of victim, altar-fire, and sanctuary;
    I hear no more sweet anthems for the wail
Of my awakened heart repenting sore.
    O bitter fruit of knowledge! Woe is me!
    Would God that I had never rent the veil!

VANQUISHED.

YEA, vanquished am I—thralled at last, and bound!
Vain, vain to strive against the Strong—all vain
The toil, the tears, the weariness, the drain
Of hot heart's blood from many a cruel wound—
Lost, lost for Earth and Heaven! But lo! I've found—
I, a veiled captive in His triumph train,
Joy that eclipseth memory of pain.
"Thy days," the world said, "run in dreary round;
Naught hast thou gained, but much hast forfeited.
Art thou not fain—speak true!—again to be

Unfettered on the flower-strewn pathway
broad?"
"Ah, tighten these dear bonds," I shuddering
said—
"My Conqueror, but not mine Enemy,
Nay, but my Friend of friends, my King,
my God!"

TRANSLATIONS.

THE WOODLAND FLOWER.

From the French of Emile Barateau.

O LITTLE woodland flower,
  Always, always hidden!
I'm seeking thee unbidden,
This many a weary hour,
To tell thee that I love thee,
That I could not prize above thee
Richest bloom of tropic bower,
My little woodland flower.

Thine artless loveliness
Wins not the trifler's smile,
Thou hast no wanton wile,
Thou breathest but to bless.

O flower drooping lowly,
Bright flower, chaste and holy,
I kiss thee, all unfearful
Of bliss with ending tearful.

The sweet bonds that unite us
Will evermore endure,
Ardent and strong and pure,—
No fears of change affright us,
I love the bird that sings to thee,
The shadow soft that brings to thee
Refreshment, flow'ret fair,—
Yea, all thy joys I share.

For oh! my maiden sweet
Hath a beloved name;
And flower, thou hast the same
I love thee, as is meet!
When she's afar I seek
Thy face so pure and meek;
Sweet flower, unto thee only,

I breathe my longings lonely.

O little woodland flower,
Always, always hidden!
I'm seeking thee unbidden,
This many a weary hour,
To tell thee that I love thee,
That I could not prize above thee
Richest bloom of tropic bower,
My little woodland flower!

WEEP NOT.

From the French.

CANST count the stars in the cloudless heaven,
    this sweet September night?
Or the snowy sails on far-off seas that against the
    storm's wrath fight?
Canst count the motes that rise and float in the
    light of one sun-ray
Or the hearts that over the sad, sad world, find
    voice to plead and pray?

God knows them all—in His sleepless love, O
    calm thy fears to rest!
He marketh the worm in its low retreat, the eagle
    in lofty nest.
Hast never heard the hymns of the birds through
    the woodland silence ring?
O think how the dear Lord guardeth thee, and
    thou, like the birds, wilt sing!

THE GOLDEN BIRD.

From the French of N. Martin.

UPON a bough with fresh-blown blossoms white,
A bird was singing in the morning light.

His eyes with glad expectancy were beaming,
His wings like sunbeams through the foliage gleaming.

Ah, me! ah, me! how did my heart prolong
The echo of the rapture of his song!

And hope grew strong in every heart that heard
The clear, sweet carol of my golden bird.

But now, he's flown afar—and must I yearn
In vain, bright bird of youth, for thy return.

THE ROSEBUSH AND THE ROSE.

From the French.

"FLOWER but at day-spring born, dost fade
    And perish with the bright day's close?
Ah! poor, frail life! fair fleeting shade!"
    Murmured the Rosebush to the Rose!

" My mother, wherefore pity me?
    Or wherefore dream the end is pain?
Sweet fragrance, blessed memory,
    I leave thee—have I lived in vain?"

GOOD-NIGHT.

From the French.

TO-MORROW, dear!
  O little word so fraught with fear!
Good-night, good-night, but will there be
Another morn for thee and me?
Perchance if Heaven revealed the morrow,
We'd part in sorrow.

Good-night, good-night!
Far from us flies the day's delight.
But now, sun-warm and lily-fair,
God's blessing lights the darkening air,
Making the ways before us bright
Good-night, good-night.

IN SANCTUARY.

AT OUR MOTHER'S SHRINE.

ANOTHER May-time cometh, sweet Mother, and I see,
Within our fair Cathedral walls, a fairer shrine for thee:—
A shrine where love hath lavished such gifts as earth can give;
A shrine where hearts in prayer will learn unto thy Son to live.

And once again, sweet Mother, thy praise I fain would sing,—
And once again, unto thy feet my lowly offering bring;
I've made for thee a garland— ah, me!—I know not why—

Behold! the flowers are fading, e'en in my hands they die!

'Tis morning yet, my Mother—see, still the East is red!

And newly gathered were the flowers, and now, alas, they're dead!

And thy image fair above me, and the image of thy Child

Look on me as in chiding, tender and grave and mild.

I have no voice to praise thee, I have no heart to pray,

Seeing the garland scattered that I wove for thee to-day;

Yet take thy blighted blossoms—smile on them, I implore,

And they will live, and bloom again, yea, sweeter than before!

Strength will return unto my heart, and song unto my lips,

And lustre to the light of joy that suffereth eclipse.
And now, e'en though I cannot pray—nor sing in praise to thee,
Here at thy feet my heart will stay, till thou remember me.

CHOSEN.

SWEET, O sweet, the voice that calling
My reluctant soul enthralling
  With unearthly melody—
Now in sleeping as in waking,
Through my dreams its music breaking,
  Seemeth thus to say to me:

Leave, O leave, thy girlhood's dreaming,
Leave the bright world's changeful seeming—
  Drop life's many-colored woof;
Leave the flowers of love to wither,
I have called—O hasten hither—
  Leave thy father's sheltering roof!

Come, beloved, I will lead thee,
And with food from Heaven feed thee,
  In the desert waste and drear;

From the noontide heats I'll shield thee,
At my word the rock will yield thee
    Living water cool and clear.

Did I ever aught to grieve thee,
Did thy hope in me deceive thee?
    Now I call thee, but in vain!
From mine arms in fear thou fleest,
In the love that claims thee, seest
    Life-long fetters, life-long pain.

 O beloved, why delayest?
Still I call, and still thou strayest,
    Wearily, so wearily—
And with pitiful endeavor,
Seekest rest that never, never,
    Wilt thou find except in me!

 1872.

CHRIST IN THE WILDERNESS

THOU has gone out from Nazareth's shelter sweet,
From Mary's mother-love, so pure, complete,
Over a long and drear and perilous way,
Into the wilderness to fast and pray.
Wherefore, my God, must all this anguish be?—
Meekly Thou answerest—"For thee, for thee."

Art Thou not weary of the desert bare—
The rock and sand and sun, the blistering air?
Were not the rivulet to Thy parched lips balm?
Yearnest Thou not for the green, sheltering palm?
Art thou not lonely, dearest Lord,—ah, me!
Though hosts of angels bear Thee company?

One slender shade is in the desert-land,
The shadow of the Cross athwart the sand:
But sharp and clear and present to Thine eyes,
The awful agonies of Calvary rise.
The Cross's shadow greateneth for me—
Ah, but the cruel nails are all for Thee!

O mystery of untold tenderness—
A boundless, shoreless sea Thy love's excess!
O I could weep methinks in Heaven above
To see my Maker pleading so for love!
Tempted and tried and sorrowing for me—
Lord, can Thy lowliest do aught for Thee?

"STAR OF MY DYING-TIME."

"Pray for us—now, and at the hour of our death."

MOTHER, the skies are dim,
    The air is cold,
And forms of terror grim
    The mists unfold.

Weary am I and weak,
    And sore afraid :—
O Virgin, pure and meek
    Sweet Mother—aid !

If I could see thy face
    'Twere almost Heaven
A sign of pitying grace
    And sin forgiven !

But O—this awful gloom
    Within, without,
The fiends of wrath and doom,
    Despair and doubt!

O for one bright hour more
    Of strength supreme,
Like those I wasted o'er
    My life's long dream!

But Mother—if thou plead
    With thy dear Son
In this, my woful need,
    My Heaven is won!

OUT OF SWEET MEMORIES.

" Quid retribuam Domino pro omnibus quæ retribuit mihi ?"

WHAT shall I render to the Lord
    For all His hand to me hath given?—
He spake—at His resistless word
    The chains that bound my heart were riven—
And even unto the Inner Shrine
He led these wandering steps of mine!

What can I give Thee?—all my love,
    The patient toil of hand and brain—
Whate'er I hold all price above
    As gathered with exceeding pain—
The slow fruition of my years
Of hope and prayer and burning tears?

What can I give?—'tis all Thine own:
    All that I am by every claim,
Is Thine, O Lord, and Thine alone
    Lent me for glory of Thy Name!
And can I look in Thy dear eyes
And count my debt—a sacrifice?

ELECTA.

ARISE, arise, my love!
  Arise, my beautiful one!—
  For the winter is over and gone,
And the voice of the turtle dove
Is already heard in the land,
And the breezes are warm and bland.

From the desert come, sweet bride;
  O rise, and haste away!
  Love brooketh no long delay,—
Then come, whatever betide.
Behold, I stand and wait
For thee at my palace-gate.

O child of my tenderest love,
  My heart goes out to thee,
  And the angel-melody

That girdles my throne above,
Is not so sweet to me there
As thy passionate human prayer.

For thee I lived and died
    I wore the crown of thorn
    That so I might adorn
Thy brow, my chosen bride,
With a crown of lilies white
Aglow with Heaven's light.

Then come, beloved, come.
    O come to my sheltering arms!
    I will soothe thy vain alarms,
And bear thee safely home.
But rise, and haste, I pray—
Love brooketh no long delay!

MY FATHER'S HOUSE.

"Lætatus sum in his quæ dicta sunt mihi: domum Domini ibimus."

THOU hast pitied my heart's great needing,
    Thou hast stooped to my low estate,
And opened unto my pleading
    The long-sealed beautiful gate.

Through the wilds of gloom and sadness,
    Thou hast been my guide and guard,
Into the light and gladness
    Of the courts of Thy house, O Lord.

Why should I fear or falter
    Under a roof so blest?
Here, near thy holy Altar,
    Surely Thy child may rest.

Here in Thy house it endeth
    My quest that was erst so vain,
For the Spirit of Peace descendeth
    Stilling the olden pain

In Thy house, my Father, never
    Is grief that burns and stings,
Nor the anguish of lost endeavor,
    Nor the shadow that chills and clings.

For Thy love makes rest of labor,
    And gain of the bitterest loss,
And the glory and joy of Thabor,
    In the shade of the drearest Cross.

A SPIRIT'S MESSAGE.

O FRIENDS on earth—O friends no longer near,
　Whom once I held, whom still I hold so dear
For Christ's sweet sake, I pray you kindly hear!

I pine—I languish in this prison-place:
O my Beloved! for one minute's space
To see again the glory of Thy Face!

Late loving! for myself I cannot pray—
Flame-girdled through the long hours I must stay,
Till the last stain of sin is burned away.

Sweet friends, I call in vain: ye answer not.
Ah, me! too well I loved you—now my lot
Is that most bitter pain—to be forgot!

For surely ye forget,—else every day
Ye would lift up pure hands to Heaven and pray
To end my long, long agony of delay!

A CHILD OF MARY'S PRAYER.

*Inscribed to the Children of Mary of St Mary's Academy,
Buffalo.*

MY own sweet Mother! oft I ve brought
    My sorrows unto thee;
And in thy love relief I've sought
    When cares pressed close on me
My humblest plaint thy pity stirred,
My feeblest prayer thy fond heart heard.

And now I come, my Mother dear,
    But not in grief or gloom;—
For lo! my life no longer drear
    Begins to bud and bloom;
And joys that ne'er were mine before
Their light through all my being pour.

With thine O let me join my song
    For I the Lord would praise
The Just, the Merciful, the Strong,
    Whose love hath blessed my days
My God, forevermore will I,
Thy Name with Mary magnify.

Yes, Mother; now to thee I bring
    My joy, as erst my woe;
And unto thee my triumph sing
    Where late my tears did flow,
And thou my happiness wilt share
Who ever heard my sorrow's prayer.

But Mother, Mother, still I fear
    This fair and cloudless sky—
I pray thee here that thou be near
    When the sweet splendors die!
For dare I hope this bliss will be
More than a flitting dream for me?

So, of my strange delight afraid,
    I trust it all to thee.
Ah, I was safer in the shade
    That once encompassed me.
O wise and tender, pure and mild,
Remember, I am still thy child.

SUMMER LILIES.

1868—1875.

WHEN midsummer's steady radiance stream-
 eth from unclouded skies,
And all fragrant, sweet, and stately, snowy summer lilies rise;
In the fervid, fruitful stillness of the noontide
 of the year,
Comes a day—thy day, O Father—to thy children
 blest, and dear.

Seven times have we watched the brightening
 of the glow of summer-tide,
Seven times have the tranquil lilies blossomed
 when the roses died,
Since God sent thee here to guide us—since with
 love and joy untold,

First we learned to greet thee, "Father," Shepherd of a favored fold.

Seven years of shine and shadow, seven years of peace and pain ;
Thine the toil and weariness, but ours the gladness and the gain.
Ah, the story of those years—the works achieved, the triumphs won—
Angels keep the splendid record in the Land beyond the sun.

May God spare thee to our needing—other prayer we dare not say—
Nobler greetings wait thy coming on this bright and blessed day.
Yet thy children trust undoubting in thy love—howe'er it be—
Lowly Nazareth's grateful tribute will not pass unmarked by thee

Rochester, July 12, 1875.

"BEHOLD, THY KING COMETH."

O DRESS thy tent with lilies and with palms,
    Robe thee in marriage-raiment white and holy
And greet His coming with rejoicing psalms,
    Who hath not scorned to choose a bride so
        lowly!

Go forth, upon His pathway gladly flinging
    All the poor treasures thou hast deemed so
        fair;
Behold! He cometh from the Orient, bringing
    Sceptre and crown for His beloved to share.

O favored one! all lesser loves forsaking
    (Frail must they seem to thee, and cold and
        dim),

Fly to thy King, nor falter, swiftly breaking
  The bonds that strive to hold thee back from
    Him.

But thou art silent; love, perchance, doth still thee
  In trance ecstatic, deepening more and more;
Yet bliss diviner draweth near to thrill thee —
  The King's bright heralds pass thy threshold
    o'er.

* * * * * * * *

Why, on thy marriage-day, in mourning languish?
  Lo, He is come at last, thy Spouse, thy King!
Why look on Him in white and wordless anguish?
  Why weep? Those tears are not love's wel-
    coming.

His sad eyes meet thine own, in mercy heeding
  Thy soul's wild agony reflected there,
Shrink'st thou because His fair white brow is bleed-
    ing

Under the royal crown His bride must share?

Shrink'st thou because His choice means pain unspoken,
    Shadows and tears, dread changes, bitter loss,
The sword unsheathed, sweet bonds forever broken?
    Shrink'st thou because His sceptre is a cross?

FORGIVEN.

SUBTLEST spells are broken,
    Firmest fetters riven;
Words of cheer, low-spoken,
    "Go in peace, forgiven."

In its pristine whiteness
    Doth my spirit shine.
Can the heart's old lightness
    E'er again be mine?

Ruthless memory hushes
    Meekest triumph now:
Tingling scarlet blushes
    Burn on cheek and brow.

O my God, my Father,
    Send me not, I pray!

Forth to battle, rather
    Bid me here to stay!

Here at Thy dear feet, Lord,
    Veiled in grief and shame,
Bearing, as is meet, Lord,
    Chastisement and blame.

Woes all thought exceeding
    Thou for me hast borne,
O Thy wide wounds bleeding
    By the scourges torn!

O the fierce derision
    Of the thorns that crowned Thee!
O Thy woful vision
    Of the foes around Thee!

Ah, send what thou wilt, Lord,
    Pain or care or loss,—
Thou hast borne my guilt, Lord,
    Help me bear its cross!

IN THANKSGIVING.

AT last! at last! O joy! O victory!
But not to me, my God, ah, not to me,
But to Thy Name the praise, the glory be!

At last! at last! but when was prayer unheeded?
And more wouldst Thou have given, had more been needed,
For purer lips than mine my cause have pleaded.

O trust, that trembled on the verge of failing!
O timid heart, at shadowy terrors quailing!
Spending thyself in conflict unavailing!

Dear God, forgive! my fears are shamed to flight;

O'ershadowed by Thy mercy and Thy might,
I rest, in humble-hearted, still delight.

O teach me song to praise Thee gladsomely,
Whose strong hands cleared the tangled way for
    me,
And saved me from the snares I could not flee!

Fain would I linger under skies so fair,
Too happy here, Lord, in my answered prayer,
To reck what stars are shining otherwhere.

SISTER MARY BERNARDINE.

In Memoriam, August 30, 1879.

I LOOKED upon thee in thy girlish sweetness,
    And thought of blights that after years
        might bring;
And wondered if thine earthly life's completeness
    Would be as blessed as its blossoming:
And prayed, with throbbing heart,—"Ah, God,
        if Thou
    Wouldst keep her evermore as she is now!"

God's answer is not always our desire—
    But mine I bend unto His gracious will;
Since He hath called thee far from me and higher,
    Yet not so high but I may reach thee still.
Blessed, beyond my dreaming, is thy share,

And yet, I know God hath not scorned my
    prayer.

And thus our ways must part. Ah, well, my way!
    Thank God that thine is not as mine, my
        sweet.
Bnt this glad thought will cheer the weariest day
    (A cooling breath in life's midsummer heat)—
My thought of angels o'er thee keeping ward,
    My lily in the garden of the Lord.

Dear child, I call thee :—I have told, dost see,
    One decade more in life's long chain of years
And much of my best life doth live in thee
    And will, when I have done with time and
        tears.
May its fruition plead with God for me,
    For what I might have been, dear, thou wilt
        be.

AN ALTAR-LAMP.

O SHINING meek and shining bright,
    An Altar-Lamp, indeed!
With ready, tender, helpful light
    For groping wanderer's need.

Without the temple-walls he stands,
    His heart is sore with sin;—
Through pictured saints' outreaching hands
    Thou beckonest him within.

Into the House of Christ the Lord,
    The wanderer's rest from roaming—
Where robe and ring and festive board
    Await his longed-for coming.

Sweet beacon-light, what joy is thine!
    I breathe, in far-off greeting;—

So near, so near the Heart Divine,
 Thou tremblest with its beating.

More joy to thee will yet be given,
 When comes the Eternal Rest;—
Christ's Altar-Lamp on earth, in Heaven
 A star upon His breast.

There, shining meek and shining bright,
 Wilt know, O fair and dear!
How many a Heavenward, leading light,
 Thy flame enkindled here?

AD MAJOREM DEI GLORIAM.

To M. E. G.

TO Thee, my God, to Thee,
   I pledge this gift of Thine, this new, bright day,
     Which dawneth glad for me—
With breeze and bloom, and bird-notes sweet and gay.

     For Thee, yea, all for Thee,
Not for the fair, frail creatures of Thy hands,
     Who erst smiled fond on me,
The while I builded high—on shifting sands.

     For Thee, my God, for Thee,
Glory or grief, soft rest, or weariness,
     What ill can come to me?
Love guides Thy hand for sword-thrust or caress.

IN SIGHT OF HOME.

THE shore's in sight, the shore's in sight!
    The longed-for lights of Home I see!
I sing for very heart's delight —
And you, my friend, thro' dark and bright,
    I know that you are glad for me.

It was a stormy voyage, friend:—
    And dare I dream the worst is o'er?
Drear presages of hapless end
Dismay me not;—yet Heaven defend!
    Ships have gone down in sight of shore.

I ought to be afraid, I know,
    My wayward past remembering;
Yet, calmly into port I go,
Whose "Sursum corda" cheers me so?
    How is it I am fain to sing?

IN SIGHT OF HOME.

Is it because my Mother stands—
    The Virgin-Mother, fair and wise—
Just where the waves break on the sands,
Reaching to me her welcoming hands,
    Lifting to God her praying eyes?

* * * * * * * *

O friend, I'm drifting from your sight—
    The Home-lights brighten momently—
Yet lift once more your signal-light,
In answer to my last good-night,
    And tell me you are glad for me!

www.ingramcontent.com/pod-product-compliance
Lightning Source LLC
Chambersburg PA
CBHW030348170426
43202CB00010B/1297